I'm so *happy*

it's happy hour

I'm so *happy*

it's happy hour

sinfully delicious cocktails

for any occasion

by

Anne Taintor

CHRONICLE BOOKS

SAN FRANCISCO

Library of Congress Cataloging-in-Publication Data
Taintor, Anne.
    I'm so happy it's happy hour: sinfully delicious cocktails for
any occasion / Anne Taintor.
        p. cm.
    ISBN 978-1-4521-0287-0 (hardcover)
    1. Cocktails. 2. Cookbooks. I. Title.
TX951.T35 2011
641.8'74—dc22

                                            2011010510

Manufactured in China

10 9 8 7 6 5 4 3 2

Chronicle Books
680 Second Street
San Francisco, California 94107
www.chroniclebooks.com

Table of Contents

INTRODUCTION 8

PIÑA COLADA 11

AVIATION 13

SOMBRERO 14

GOODY TWO-SHOES 17

WHISTLING GYPSY 19

PINK PUSSYCAT 20

MERRY WIDOW 23

GIN AND SIN 25

BRAZEN HUSSY 26

PINK SQUIRREL VS. TOM COLLINS 28

GOLFER 31

EL PRESIDENTE 33

STUPID CUPID 34

NO SAINT 37

NAKED WAITER 39

QUEEN BEE 40

SCARLET LADY 43

ORIGINAL SIN 45

SLINKY MINK 46

PILLOW TALK 49

HELLO SAILOR 51

ZOMBIE 52

SAYONARA 55

3 A.M. ON A SCHOOL NIGHT 57

ABSINTHE MINDED 58

DIRTY GIRL SCOUT 61

ROAD RUNNER 63

GRASSHOPPER 64

DAVID'S HENDRICK'S MARTINI 67

CLASSIC COSMOPOLITAN 69

FROZEN WATERMELON DAIQUIRI 70

GIN RICKEY 73

FROZEN MUDSLIDE 75

PICKLEBACK 76

BEST IN SHOW 79

PECKERHEAD 81

LADY OF LEISURE 82

SWISS COFFEE 85

GRETA GARBO 87

MOJITO 88

DIAMOND RING 91

FROSTBITE 93

INDEX 94

TABLE OF EQUIVALENTS 96

Introduction

I grew up with a proper reverence for cocktails. My grandfather used to sit on the back steps with his next-door neighbor and a couple of cocktails. They called this their "hour of charm." Every day when my father came home from work, he and my mother took their cocktails into the sunroom and sent us kids outside. Nothing was ever more exciting than peeking from the top of the staircase when my parents invited in a houseful of friends for a few shakerfuls.

When, as a young adult, I was finally able to drink cocktails *myself*, I made one or two slight errors in judgment. As a matter of self-preservation, I adopted the "never mix, never worry" approach to drinking and became for many years a one-drink gal. Oh, the wasted years!

My friend Martha once told me that after three martinis (my one drink), I find myself very amusing. So as I tested cocktails for inclusion in this collection, I endeavored to limit myself to two per evening . . . not as easy as it sounds!

Who knew there was such a big delicious world of cocktails beyond my (still beloved) Hendrick's martini? The Merry Widow cocktail is a new personal favorite; every time I drink one, I feel as though I'm wearing pearls and heels. (Believe me, I'm not.) The Frostbite was a monumental success at the Taintor family Christmas reunion. Against all odds, my six-foot-five, leather-clad nephew has become a *huge* fan of the Pink

Squirrel. I look forward wistfully to a long summer of Naked Waiters on my patio. And the Scarlet Lady? Any cocktail featuring Campari is a winner in my book.

You know what they say about nice work if you can get it? Putting this collection together was the nicest work I ever got! I sincerely hope that you will enjoy every one of these cocktails just as much as I did.

Cheers!

Piña Colada

Who has not, when in a festive mood, put an umbrella in her martini? But the very best drink in which to put an umbrella is the classic piña colada.

....

2 ounces light rum

2 ounces cream of coconut

1 ounce coconut milk

1 ounce pineapple juice

⅛ cup chopped pineapple

1½ cups crushed ice

Pineapple wedge for garnish

....

Mix the liquid ingredients and the chopped pineapple in a blender with the crushed ice at high speed until smooth. Pour into a hurricane glass. Garnish with a pineapple wedge . . . and an umbrella.

think of me as

"unexpected turbulence"

Aviation

They used to call it "unexpected turbulence," a phrase fraught with suggestion. Now they call it "rough air." No wonder they say air travel has lost its glamour! Create a little "unexpected turbulence" of your own with this glamorous classic cocktail.

....

2½ ounces gin

½ ounce maraschino liqueur

½ ounce lemon juice

Ice cubes

Maraschino cherry for garnish

....

Shake the liquid ingredients vigorously with ice and strain into a chilled martini glass. Garnish with a maraschino cherry.

Sombrero

Nuance is everything. "Adios" and "hasta luego"? Kind of the same . . . and yet oh so different. Many years ago I worked in a bar, and I served five hundred million Sombreros. The Sombreros we served were coffee liqueur and milk over ice. People seemed to like them, but I think you will find this cocktail much more nuanced.

....

1 ounce pure agave tequila

1 ounce coffee liqueur

2 teaspoons créme de cacao

4 ounces light cream

Ice cubes

Grated nutmeg for garnish

....

Shake the liquid ingredients vigorously with ice and strain into a chilled old-fashioned glass. Sprinkle with grated nutmeg.

Goody Two-Shoes

If you spend too long hanging around with nuns (say, for instance, in your eight years of Catholic school), you run the very real risk of turning into a goody two-shoes. Don't despair! With a little creative drinking, you'll kick off those shoes in no time! This yummy cocktail should help.

....

1 ounce dark rum

1 ounce peach schnapps

1 ounce coconut liqueur

1 ounce pineapple juice

1 ounce orange juice

Ice cubes

Pineapple wedge for garnish

....

Shake the liquid ingredients vigorously with ice and strain into a large cocktail glass. Garnish with a pineapple wedge.

she was

one cocktail away

from proving

his mother right

Whistling Gypsy

My first mother-in-law used to refer to me, I am told, as "that gypsy." Guess what I called her?

1 ounce Tia Maria

1 ounce Baileys Irish Cream

1 ounce vodka

Pour the Tia Maria into a double shot glass. Using the back of a spoon, slowly float the Baileys Irish Cream, and then the vodka, in that order.

Pink Pussycat

If what you're looking for in a relationship is charm, maturity, and honest affection, you may be looking for a cat. If what you're looking for in a cocktail is fruity and delicious, look no further.

2 ounces gin

4 ounces pineapple juice

Ice cubes

1 teaspoon grenadine

Combine the gin and the pineapple juice in an old-fashioned glass almost filled with ice cubes. Stir well. Drop the grenadine into the center of the drink.

Merry Widow

My daughter was ten when she made the observation that I seemed to prefer imaginary men. Not all the time! But who among us has not fantasized on occasion about an empty armchair, a silent television set, and a nice quiet cocktail alone.

....

1 ounce gin

1 ounce sweet vermouth

½ ounce Bénédictine

½ ounce pastis

Dash of bitters

Ice cubes

Lemon twist for garnish

....

Shake the liquid ingredients vigorously with ice and strain into a chilled cocktail glass. Garnish with a lemon twist.

Gin and Sin

I've never understood what's so sinful about citrus juice. Maybe the sin is that this cocktail can so easily be mistaken for a breakfast beverage.

1½ ounces gin

1 ounce orange juice

1 ounce lemon juice

½ teaspoon grenadine

Ice cubes

Shake the liquid ingredients vigorously with ice and strain into a chilled cocktail glass.

Brazen Hussy

All too often you have to look "professional." There are times you may have to look elegant. But there are other, glorious times—thank God—when only cheap will do. And nothing says "I'm cheap" like shaking up a batch of Brazen Hussies for your pals.

1½ ounces vodka

1½ ounces triple sec

Splash of lemon juice

Ice cubes

Lemon wedge for garnish

Shake the liquid ingredients vigorously with ice and strain into a chilled cocktail glass. Garnish with a lemon wedge.

Pink Squirrel vs. Tom Collins

No euphemisms are necessary for cocktails as delicious as these.

....

Tom Collins

2 ounces gin

1 ounce lemon juice

1 teaspoon superfine sugar

Ice cubes

3 ounces club soda

Maraschino cherry for garnish

Orange slice for garnish

....

Shake the gin, lemon juice, and sugar with ice and strain into a collins glass. Add the club soda and garnish with a maraschino cherry and an orange slice.

if you show me your Pink Squirrel

I'll show you

my Tom Collins

Pink Squirrel

CASTLETYMON BRANCH PH. 4524888

1 ounce light cream

1 ounce white crème de cacao

1 ounce crème de noyaux

Ice cubes

Shake the liquid ingredients vigorously with ice and strain into a chilled cocktail glass.

she had told him that she liked to swing

Golfer

. . . and boy, was he disappointed when she clarified her statement!

1½ ounces vodka

1½ ounces gin

Dash of dry vermouth

Ice cubes

Lemon twist for garnish

Stir the liquid ingredients with ice in a mixing glass and strain into a chilled cocktail glass. Garnish with a lemon twist.

El Presidente

My favorite non-apology ever, and the favorite non-apology of many, many American presidents! Shake up a round or two of these and make a few mistakes of your own.

....

2 ounces light rum

1 tablespoon pineapple juice

1 teaspoon grenadine

1 tablespoon lime juice

Ice cubes

Orange twist for garnish

....

Shake the liquid ingredients vigorously with ice and strain into a chilled cocktail glass. Garnish with an orange twist.

Stupid Cupid

Who among us has not committed some insanity at the urging of this stupid little Roman god? And why is such a charming cocktail named after such an annoying little twerp?

....

1 ounce citrus-flavored vodka

½ ounce sloe gin

1 ounce lime juice

½ ounce simple syrup

Ice cubes

....

Shake the liquid ingredients vigorously with ice and strain into a chilled cocktail glass.

No Saint

Angelic is for six-year-olds. We're grown women, for heaven's sake!

....

1½ ounces vodka

1½ ounces orange juice

Dash of dry vermouth

Dash of bitters

Ice cubes

....

Shake the liquid ingredients vigorously with ice and strain into a chilled cocktail glass.

Naked Waiter

We all enjoy men who enjoy taking orders. Many of us enjoy naked men. A drink named after a naked man taking orders has got to be a winner.

3 ounces lemonade

1 ounce Mandarine Napoleon

1 ounce pastis

1 ounce pineapple juice

Ice cubes

Lemon slice for garnish

Pour the liquid ingredients over ice in a highball glass and stir. Garnish with a lemon slice.

Queen Bee

If you were a bee, you'd be the queen bee, right? So what's with all the cooking and cleaning? Shake up a batch of queen bees, put your feet up, and reign.

....

¾ ounce honey

¾ ounce lemon juice

¾ ounce pineapple juice

1½ ounces vodka

¾ ounce St. Germain elderflower liquor

Ice cubes

Splash of prosecco or other sparkling dry white wine

....

Whisk the honey with the lemon juice and pineapple juice until it dissolves. Shake vigorously with the vodka, St. Germain, and ice and strain into a chilled cocktail glass. Top with a splash of prosecco.

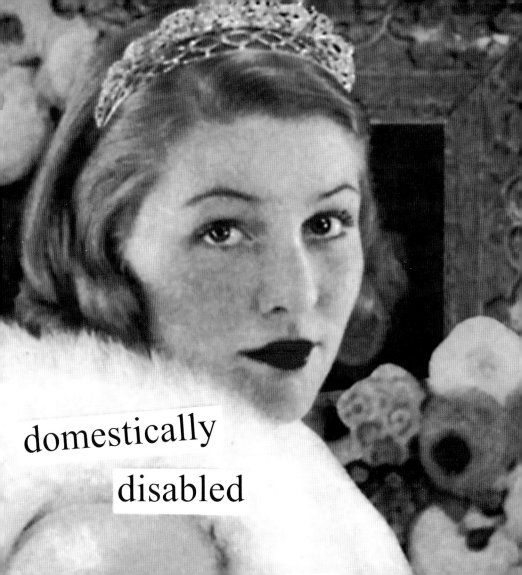

domestically disabled

Scarlet Lady

Life can be very confusing. Make the wrong choice just one time and you may find you've earned yourself a reputation. The Scarlet Lady is a lot like life: a little bitter, a little sweet . . . absolutely delightful!

```
1 ounce Campari

1 ounce Mandarine Napoleon

Splash of grenadine

Splash of lime juice

Ice cubes

Lime twist for garnish
```

Shake the liquid ingredients vigorously with ice and strain into a chilled cocktail glass. Garnish with a lime twist.

she had

not yet decided

whether

to use

her power

for good…

or for evil

Original Sin

Good . . . or evil? Good . . . or evil? Hmm . . . it can sometimes be a very tough decision. Often a refreshing cocktail or two helps me decide.

2 ounces Champagne

1 ounce brandy

Splash of triple sec

Splash of grenadine

Orange twist for garnish

Pour the liquid ingredients into a brandy snifter and stir. Garnish with an orange twist.

Slinky Mink

Minimalism has its place. A simple glass of Champagne, for example, is very, very nice. But the Slinky Mink is a little "more" . . . and it's perfect.

....

½ ounce raspberry puree

2 teaspoons lime juice

Dash of simple syrup

Champagne

Lime twist for garnish

....

Pour the raspberry puree, lime juice, and simple syrup into a chilled Champagne flute. Top up with Champagne and stir gently. Garnish with a lime twist.

whoever said
"less is more"
had probably
never
had
quite enough "more"

Pillow Talk

Ah, the morning after! Generally preceded by the evening before. And possibly by a few of these smooth, sweet shots.

1 ounce chilled strawberry vodka

1 ounce white chocolate liqueur

Dollop of whipped cream

Pour the vodka into a shot glass. Using the back of a spoon, slowly float the white chocolate liqueur over the vodka. Top with the whipped cream.

Hello Sailor

Tattoos: not just for sailors anymore.

....

1 ounce spiced rum

¾ ounce golden rum

⅓ ounce Pedro Ximénez sherry

⅓ ounce orange liqueur

½ ounce lemon juice

½ ounce lime juice

Ice cubes

Orange twist for garnish

....

Shake the liquid ingredients vigorously with ice and strain into a
chilled cocktail glass. Garnish with an orange twist.

Zombie

I assure you . . . there will be side effects.

....

1 ounce dark rum

1 ounce light rum

½ ounce golden rum

½ ounce apricot brandy

Juice of ½ lime

1 teaspoon grenadine

⅓ ounce pineapple juice

½ ounce simple syrup

Ice cubes

⅓ ounce overproof rum

Pineapple wedge for garnish

....

Shake all of the liquid ingredients except the overproof rum vigorously with ice. Pour into a highball or tiki glass without straining. Using the back of a spoon, float the overproof rum on top. Garnish with a pineapple wedge.

it would,

of course,

have to look

like an accident

Sayonara

A wise man once said there must be fifty ways to leave your lover. An "accident" is one tried and true method . . . but just saying "sayonara" is less risky. Whichever method you choose, celebrate afterward with this refreshing cocktail.

1½ ounces gin

1 ounce sake

½ ounce triple sec

Ice cubes

Orange twist to garnish

Shake the liquid ingredients vigorously with ice and strain into a chilled cocktail glass. Garnish with an orange twist.

why yes, I *am* that kind of girl

3A.M. on a School Night

To that kind of girl there's no such thing as too much, too many, or too late.

....

6 ounces fruit punch

1½ ounces light rum

1 ounce vodka

¼ ounce amaretto

¼ ounce apricot brandy

Ice cubes

....

Shake the liquid ingredients vigorously with ice and strain into a highball glass.

Absinthe Minded

Contrary to popular belief, absinthe (at least in my opinion) is an unusually lucid high. Have a couple of these the next time you need to take a message.

....

2 ounces absinthe

Dash of lemon juice

Dash of raspberry liqueur

Ice cubes

....

Shake the liquid ingredients briefly with ice and strain into a chilled shot glass.

Dirty Girl Scout

It's a lucky lady who has never been cajoled into spending the night in a sleeping bag in the godforsaken woods somewhere. But the Dirty Girl Scout is as at home around the campfire (no chilled cocktail glasses required!) as she is in the living room. Don't leave your tent without one.

1 ounce peppermint schnapps

1½ ounces Kahlua

2½ ounces chocolate milk

Ice cubes

Shake the liquid ingredients vigorously with ice and strain into an ice-filled old-fashioned glass.

Road Runner

Cocktails go with road trips like Thelma goes with Louise. Make sure you have a designated driver.

....

1½ ounces vodka

¾ ounce amaretto

¾ ounce coconut milk

Ice cubes

Grated nutmeg for garnish

....

Shake the liquid ingredients vigorously with ice. Strain into a chilled cocktail glass. Sprinkle with grated nutmeg.

Grasshopper

This is a drink I wish had come with a warning label. I was twenty years old and quite inexperienced as far as liquor was concerned. I was at a wedding rehearsal dinner—mine. Someone gave me a Grasshopper . . . and then another . . . and another . . . and another. They tell me I got married the next day. I don't remember.

....

1 ounce white crème de cacao

1 ounce crème de menthe

1 ounce light cream

Ice cubes

Mint sprig for garnish

....

Shake the liquid ingredients vigorously with ice and strain into a chilled cocktail glass. Garnish with a mint sprig.

Don't drink too many.

David's Hendrick's Martini

Gordon's is fine in a gin and tonic, but for a martini the gin has to be Hendrick's. A friend introduced me to this Hendrick's martini . . . with sake in place of the dry vermouth.

....

3 ounces Hendrick's gin

2½ teaspoons sake

Ice cubes

Thin cucumber slice for garnish

....

Shake the liquid ingredients with really fresh ice and strain into a chilled martini glass. Okay, okay . . . you can stir it if you must. Garnish with a thin cucumber slice.

suddenly
she even
felt
cosmopolitan

Classic Cosmopolitan

Classic is as classic does.

....

1 ounce vodka

½ ounce triple sec

½ ounce lime juice

½ ounce cranberry juice

Ice cubes

Lime wedge for garnish

....

Shake the liquid ingredients with ice and strain into a chilled cocktail glass. Garnish with a lime wedge.

Frozen Watermelon Daiquiri

And why do regular old daiquiris when you can do these?

1½ ounces white rum

¾ ounce lime juice

1 cup seeded, chopped watermelon

¼ cup lime sorbet

½ cup crushed ice

Lime slice for garnish

Mix the liquid ingredients, watermelon, and lime sorbet in a blender with the crushed ice at high speed until smooth. Pour into a chilled cocktail glass. Garnish with a lime slice.

Gin Rickey

And what an easy way to polish it off! The only easier way to drink gin is straight from the bottle.

....

2 ounces gin

1 ounce lime juice

5 ounces club soda

Ice cubes

Lime wedge for garnish

....

Pour the liquid ingredients over ice in a highball glass and stir. Garnish with a lime wedge.

Frozen Mudslide

A very wise man once said, "Candy is dandy, but liquor is quicker." With this cocktail you get the best of both worlds: sweet as any chocolate bar . . . and fast-acting!

2 cups crushed ice

¾ ounce vodka

¾ ounce Kahlua

¾ ounce Baileys Irish Cream

1 tablespoon chocolate syrup

¼ cup whipped cream

In a blender combine ice, vodka, Kahlua, and Baileys. Drizzle with chocolate syrup. Blend until smooth and pour into a margarita glass. Top with the whipped cream.

Pickleback

In Poland, drinking dill pickle juice, which is full of antioxidants, healing salts, and minerals, is a traditional cure for the common hangover. Disgusting as it may sound, this drink is actually quite delicious.

```
1 shot good-quality Irish Whiskey
1 shot good-quality dill pickle juice
```

Drink the whiskey. Now drink the pickle juice.

Best in Show

Puppies, quick to commit and needy as hell, also make excellent rebound partners.

....

1½ ounces dark rum

1½ ounces apricot liqueur

1½ ounces cola

Splash of grenadine

Ice cubes

....

Stir the liquid ingredients vigorously with ice and strain into a chilled cocktail glass.

she threw
herself
eagerly
into
the paths
of unsuitable men

Peckerhead

A friend once told me that this caption sparked an empowering revelation for her. She suddenly understood that she was in control of her "love life." She was the one throwing herself at these hopelessly unsuitable men, and the men weren't doing anything at all except being themselves . . . peckerheads.

....

1½ ounces orange juice

¾ ounce Southern Comfort

¾ ounce vodka

¾ ounce sloe gin

Splash of lime juice

Ice cubes

....

Shake the liquid ingredients vigorously with ice and strain into a chilled cocktail glass.

Lady of Leisure

Just thinking about Monday morning—and the five million e-mails that will surely demand your immediate attention—can drive you to drink. Some day we'll be ladies of leisure . . . and have even more time to drink.

....

1 ounce gin

½ ounce raspberry liqueur

¼ ounce Cointreau

1 ounce pineapple juice

Dash of lemon juice

Ice cubes

Orange twist for garnish

....

Shake the liquid ingredients vigorously with ice and strain into a chilled cocktail glass. Garnish with an orange twist.

if only Monday morning were as easy as I am…

Swiss Coffee

As those with years of experience know, you can pour virtually any type of alcohol into a cup of coffee and come up with a winner . . . but this combo is especially nice. One or two of these and any interruptions to your "coffee break" will roll right off you.

4 ounces premium, dark roast, medium-ground coffee

1 ounce Kahlua

1 ounce amaretto

1 ounce Tia Maria

1 ounce dark crème de cacao

Dollop of whipped cream

Stir together liquid ingredients in a heat-proof glass. Top with the whipped cream.

Greta Garbo

Spending a day alone always brings me back to center. Sleeping alone can be an absolute delight. And the pleasures of drinking alone have been extolled by wise men from Li Po to George Thorogood. Try it just this once.

```
2 ounces light rum
Splash of maraschino liqueur
Splash of lime juice
Splash of pastis
Pinch of sugar
Ice cubes
```

Shake the liquid ingredients and the sugar vigorously with ice and strain into a chilled cocktail glass.

Mojito

A mojito is a terrific way to get your RDAs when you just can't get to the salad bar.

. . . .

8 mint leaves

½ lime, cut into wedges

1 tablespoon sugar

1 cup crushed ice

2 ounces rum

4 ounces club soda

Mint sprig for garnish

Lime wedge for garnish

. . . .

Muddle the mint leaves, lime wedges, and sugar in a highball glass. Fill the glass with the crushed ice and add the rum. Stir and top with club soda. Garnish with a mint sprig and a lime wedge.

she still missed

those

yuppie eastern greens

now that he had bought the cow, the milk was going to be *extraordinarily* expensive

Diamond Ring

The diamond ring is just the beginning.

....

Dash of boiling water

1 teaspoon clear honey

3 basil leaves

1½ ounces vodka

1 ounce apple juice

Ice cubes

Apple slice for garnish

....

Stir the water, honey, and basil leaves together in a shaker until well blended. Add the vodka, apple juice, and a few ice cubes. Shake vigorously and strain into a chilled martini glass. Garnish with an apple slice.

hell yeah, I've been naughty!

Frostbite

He already knows you've been naughty, so drop the nice girl act and shake up a serving of Frostbite.

....

1 ounce tequila

1 ounce heavy cream

1 ounce white crème de cacao

½ ounce white crème de menthe

Ice cubes

Cocoa powder for garnish

....

Shake the liquid ingredients vigorously with ice and strain into a chilled cocktail glass. Sprinkle with cocoa powder for garnish.

Index

ABSINTHE
Absinthe Minded, 58

AMARETTO
3 A.M. on a School Night, 57
Road Runner, 63
Swiss Coffee, 85

APRICOT BRANDY
3 A.M. on a School
    Night, 57
Zombie, 52

APRICOT LIQUEUR
Best in Show, 79

BAILEY'S IRISH CREAM
(see Irish cream liqueur)

BÉNÉDICTINE
Merry Widow, 23

BRANDY
(see also individual brandies)
Original Sin, 45

CAMPARI
Scarlet Lady, 43

**CHAMPAGNE AND
SPARKLING WINES**
Original Sin, 45

Slinky Mink, 46
Queen Bee, 40

CITRUS VODKA
Stupid Cupid, 34

COCONUT LIQUOR
Goody Two-Shoes, 17

COFFEE LIQUEUR
Sombrero, 14

COINTREAU
Lady of Leisure, 82

CRÈME DE CACAO
Frostbite, 93
Grasshopper, 64
Pink Squirrel, 29
Sombrero, 14
Swiss Coffee, 85

CRÈME DE MENTHE
Frostbite, 93
Grasshopper, 64

CRÈME DE NOYAUX
Pink Squirrel, 29

ELDERFLOWER LIQUOR
(see St. Germain)

GIN
Aviation, 13
David's Hendrick's Martini
    (Hendrick's), 63
Gin and Sin, 25
Gin Rickey, 73
Golfer, 31
Lady of Leisure, 82
Merry Widow, 82
Pink Pussycat, 20
Sayonara, 55
Tom Collins, 28

IRISH CREAM LIQUOR
Frozen Mudslide, 75
Whistling Gypsy, 19

KAHLÚA
Dirty Girl Scout, 61
Frozen Mudslide, 75
Swiss Coffee, 85

**MANDARINE NAPOLEON
LIQUEUR**
Naked Waiter, 39
Scarlet Lady, 43

MARASCHINO LIQUEUR
Aviation, 13
Greta Garbo, 87

PASTIS
Greta Garbo, 87
Merry Widow, 23
Naked Waiter, 39

PEACH SCHNAPPS
Goody Two-Shoes, 17

PEDRO XIMÉNEZ
Hello Sailor, 51

PEPPERMINT SCHNAPPS
Dirty Girl Scout, 61

RASPBERRY LIQUEUR
Absinthe Minded, 58
Lady of Leisure, 82

RUM
3 A.M. on a School
    Night, 57
Best in Show, 79
El Presidente, 33
Frozen Watermelon
    Daiquiri, 70
Goody Two-Shoes, 17
Greta Garbo, 87
Hello Sailor, 51
Mojito, 88
Pina Colada, 11
Zombie, 52

SAKE
Sayonara, 55
David's Hendrick's
    Martini, 67

SLOE GIN
Peckerhead, 81
Stupid Cupid, 34

SOUTHERN COMFORT
Peckerhead, 81

ST. GERMAIN
Queen Bee, 40

STRAWBERRY VODKA
Pillow Talk, 49

TEQUILA
Sombrero, 14
Frostbite, 93

TIA MARIA
Swiss Coffee, 85
Whistling Gypsy, 19

TRIPLE SEC
Brazen Hussy, 26
Classic Cosmopolitan, 69
Hello Sailor, 51
Original Sin, 45
Sayonara, 55

VERMOUTH
Golfer, 33
No Saint, 37
Merry Widow, 23

VODKA
(see also individual flavors)
3 A.M. on a School
    Night, 57
Brazen Hussy, 26
Classic Cosmopolitan, 69
Diamond Ring, 91
Frozen Mudslide, 75
Golfer, 31
No Saint, 37
Peckerhead, 81
Pillow Talk, 49
Queen Bee, 40
Road runner, 63
Stupid Cupid, 34
Whistling Gypsy, 19

WHISKEY
Pickleback, 76

**WHITE CHOCOLATE
LIQUEUR**
Pillow Talk, 49

Table of Equivalents

1 TEASPOON	**⅙ OUNCE**	
½ TABLESPOON	**¼ OUNCE**	
2 TEASPOONS	**⅓ OUNCE**	
1 TABLESPOON	**½ OUNCE**	
1 ½ TABLESPOONS	**¾ OUNCE**	
2 TABLESPOONS (⅛ CUP)	**1 OUNCE**	
3 TABLESPOONS (SHOT)	**1 ½ OUNCES**	
¼ CUP	**2 OUNCES**	**60 MILLILITERS**
⅓ CUP	**2 ½ OUNCES**	**75 MILLILITERS**
⅜ CUP	**3 OUNCES**	**90 MILLILITERS**
½ CUP	**4 OUNCES**	**120 MILLILITERS**
⅔ CUP	**5 OUNCES**	**150 MILLILITERS**
1 CUP	**8 OUNCES**	**240 MILLILITERS**

1 CUP CRUSHED ICE	**150 GRAMS**
1 CUP CUBED WATERMELON	**170 GRAMS**